Istanbul.

A city of contradictions divided by a strait which continues to grow despite its political and economic woes. Endearingly chaotic, the giant Turkish cosmopolis is as historic and nostalgic as it is modern and young.

The city's main source of inspiration is the entrepreneurial spirit of its young people who bestow the city's ancient narrative with new life. Old neoclassical city apartments have become ateliers, art galleries and concept stores, former Bosphorus homes are now three-floor restaurants or cocktail bars with a view. From the wealthy Bosphorus coast down through the urbane backstreets of Beyoglu, to the more bohemian Moda, every neighborhood has its own story and spirit, gaining new purpose with the influx of youthful creativity.

In Istanbul we spoke to a young musician who is reinterpreting classical Turkish music with rock & roll, a drag queen who knows Istanbul's nightlife inside and out, a chef who scours the country for the best ingredients, a designer who's bringing back the vintage gentleman look and a musician and entrepreneur couple. It's easy to get lost in and fall in love with Istanbul.

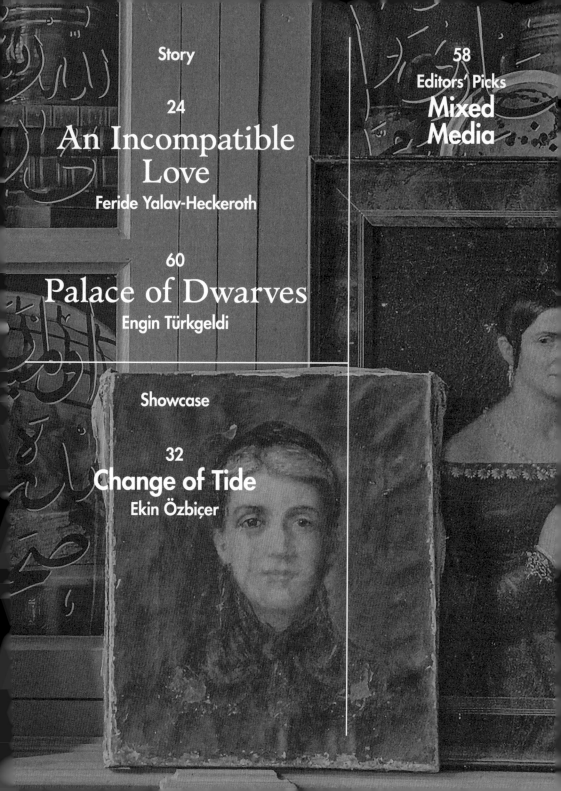

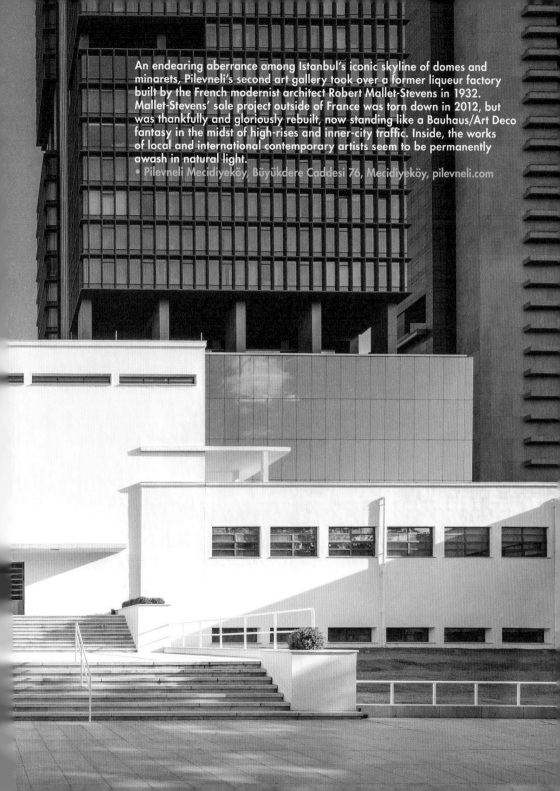

An endearing aberrance among Istanbul's iconic skyline of domes and minarets, Pilevneli's second art gallery took over a former liqueur factory built by the French modernist architect Robert Mallet-Stevens in 1932. Mallet-Stevens' sole project outside of France was torn down in 2012, but was thankfully and gloriously rebuilt, now standing like a Bauhaus/Art Deco fantasy in the midst of high-rises and inner-city traffic. Inside, the works of local and international contemporary artists seem to be permanently awash in natural light.
• Pilevneli Mecidiyeköy, Büyükdere Caddesi 76, Mecidiyeköy, pilevneli.com

Street Food Elite

There was nothing particularly glamorous about Turkish street food until the chefs of *Alaf* came along and made it gourmet, even slightly upscale. Classics like kokoreç (chopped lamb intestines), iskembe (tripe soup) or uykuluk (sweetbread) are enhanced through quality ingredients and an experimental approach to taste combinations and presentation. The Alaf eatery is open for lunch with a few daily dishes, while for dinner, the upstairs dining room has a longer menu and a Bosphorus view.
• Alaf, Kuruçesme Caddesi 19, Arnavkutköy, alafkurucesme.com

From Lamb Intestines to Underground Clubbing

Capital of the World

Culture | Relentlessly Clean

Inspired by ancient Roman bathing practices, the Turkish Bath has been a fixture of relaxation and cleansing since the Ottoman Empire. Tourists love getting scrubbed and vigorously washed at one of Istanbul's many historic hamams. For something a little less touristy, the beautifully renovated *Çukurcuma Hamamı* only accommodates four people at a time, which is a boon in terms of being scrubbed, washed and massaged in a more private environment.
• Çukurcuma Hamamı, Çukurcuma Caddesi 43, Beyoglu, cukurcumahamami.com

8

Food The Meyhane Experience

To simply compare a meyhane to a tavern is a slight insult given how vital these particular restaurants are to the fabric of Istanbul's identity. A meyhane is a place to eat meze and drink raki, but more so, it's the guardian of Istanbul's past and a place for friendship to be deepened and conversation liberated by sweet inebriation. A meyhane that dates back to 1895, *Safa Meyhanesi* (pictured) is as classic as it gets, with a large antique chandelier, vintage Kulüp Rakı bottles, posters and amazing traditional meze. Another eternal meyhane that's on a secluded side street deep in the Bomonti neighborhood, *Madam Despina'nın Meyhanesi* was the first tavern to be opened by a woman in 1946, and her portrait at the entrance stands as evidence to the fact. Madam Despina's topik (Armenian chickpea dish with onions, currants, and nuts) and yaprak cigeri (sliced liver) match perfectly with some glasses of raki.

• Various locations

A la Turca Home

As a city that's hosted various empires and cultures, stores selling antique home objects and crafts are plentiful in Istanbul, but only a few have collections that are worth their price. Kasif Gündogdu and Sonay Özön are two of the city's most respected antiques dealers and their shops *Sofa Art & Antiques* and *Samdan* can be found in Galata and Çukurcuma respectively. *Dada Kuzguncuk* (pictured) is another worthy antique shop, which regularly changes its theme and decks out its store with rare finds from its depot in Tuzla. In Sultanahmet, look no further than *Dhoku and Ethnicon* for vintage or modern carpets and *Iznik Classics* for hand-painted Iznik tiles and objects.
• Various locations

Night Down and Dirty

Contrary to popular belief, Istanbul's nightlife is still alive and growing, although its more uninhibited dance parties tend to unfold in the shadows at more underground venues. Situated in a renovated building built in 1902, *Suma Han* (pictured) is a kind of artists' commune that hosts exhibitions and events, and, more importantly, some of the city's best DJ parties. Another important stop for electronic music is *Module*, a little outside the city centre, which often features international DJs on an 8-hour-plus party basis.
• Various locations

Outdoors **Island Hopping**

Istanbul's islands are a popular getaway destination, and can easily be reached via ferries that depart from both sides of the Bosphorus. A good tip is to avoid Büyükada (the biggest island) and its weekend/holiday crowds, and rather head to the less popular but equally fascinating island of Burgazada. If you get there early enough, order breakfast and a downright excellent cup of coffee at *Four Letter Word Coffee*, do some shopping at the tiny design boutique *3 Things on an Island*, and hike up to the peak to visit the Hristos Tepesi and its historic monastery where the view is a thing of pure serenity. For a lunch of Turkish classics, take the scenic walk to *Kalpazankaya* and grab a table facing the sparkling seascape.
• Various locations

Outdoors **Tea Time**

Ubiquitous all over Istanbul and especially enjoyable whilst riding the ferry from one continent to the other, Turkish tea is probably more popular than water. The çay bahçesi (Turkish tea garden) came to life in the 1950s and, unlike its Japanese counterpart, has always been a social venue for loud conversations to be had and kids to run around in. The *Moda Çay Bahçesi* is not really a formal establishment but rather a small secret garden with a few tiny Anatolian-style wooden tables and endless servings of Turkish tea (only). The other thing that attracts people here is the sea view, especially at sunset.
• Moda Çay Bahçesi, Küçükmoda Burnu Sokak, Kadıköy

Gaye Su Akyol, Musician

Free Spirit

A rollicking force in the young contemporary Turkish music scene, Akyol is a Kadıköy local who basks in the nostalgia of her neighbourhood. Here she takes time out of her busy schedule to share some old-school favourites, places where she discovers new music, and her style icon Zeki Müren

How has Kadıköy shaped you as a musician?

I was born in Kadıköy, spent my whole life here and even lived on the same street for 23 years. So I can say that Kadıköy conjures a very deep and meaningful response within me, it's my home base, so to speak. Kadıköy's long history has definitely influenced me. This neighbourhood has seen so many different cultures and has been the place where many artists, painters and musicians were born and raised. It's also Kadıköy's subculture that's been a big part of my life, the rock and roll scene, the record stores in the Akmar Pasajı, the way that people come here to listen to good music and to hang out freely. All of that influenced me. Ever since I discovered my identity and realized I was different, Kadıköy became a place that accepted me and shaped my music, a place where I felt free.

What are some of your favourite venues in Kadıköy that have stood the test of time?

For the old-school stuff, I would say *Koço Restaurant*, for drinking raki, and the *Hacı Bekir* shop where you can always eat something sweet. There's *Arkaoda* bar and their new place *Bina*, which we go to frequently for the good people, good concerts and good conversation. Bina has also become a place for cultural exchange thanks to a collaboration with Bant Mag. There's the *Sürreya Cinema*, which became an opera house, and we really like going to the *Moda Sahnesi* theatre, which is run by a few of our close friends. The *Rexx Cinema* has maintained its old-school vibes and the Moda Sahil boardwalk is always a good bet. I also really like the Akmar Pasajı arcade, it evokes a nostalgic feeling, especially downstairs with all its

CDs and records, it's just a great place to find old recordings.

Any favourites on the European side?

Well, there's the *Yakup* meyhane and the Hazzopulo Pasajı arcade, which I love.

You have some very elaborate stage costumes, where do you go shopping?

I shop at flea markets and second-hand shops wherever I go, but at the moment, it's become more of a styling process where I sketch out my costumes and work with tailors to have them made. So, kind of what Zeki Müren did back in the day.

So Zeki Müren is an inspiration to you?

Zeki Müren is a true diva and a true style icon. He was at the top of his class while studying design at the Mimar Sinan Fine Arts University and he created all his own costumes. I feel we have a lot of things in common. He was a revisionist who changed classic Turkish music despite the teachers and experts who rejected him. He was like the David Bowie of his era, or David Bowie was like the Zeki Müren of his era. He changed a lot of things and broke a lot of rules, and so many people followed him.

Where do you go to check out new music?

If you'd asked me a few years ago I would have said Peyote. At the moment, there are a bunch of new places opening up in Kadıköy. *Bina* is one of them, they host mini-concerts on the top floor. There's also *Mecra*, which is similar to Bina, a bar with a performance and events space. *Naya*, a reggae bar from the European side, opened up in Kadıköy, and they've begun to host different genres of music such as punk.

There's nothing mixed up about the above-par exhibitions at Mixer, which focus exclusively on emerging local talent

Moda Tea Garden
Moda

Pg Art Gallery
Beyoglu

Mixer
Karaköy

What do you when you have some time off from performing and touring?

Well, being able to ride the ferry to the other side of Istanbul is an amazing comfort. But at the moment, we're spending a lot of time on our terrace at home, to be honest. Or at the *Moda Tea Garden*, with a view of the boardwalk. The Kalamıs neighbourhood is also a great place to explore, as well as Kuzguncuk and Beykoz. My grandmother had a summer home in Beykoz and we used to go there a lot. When I have some more time and energy I want to go there again.

You have a background in painting, do you have any favourite galleries?

I follow *Pg Art Gallery* and there's always something good at *Mixer*. Tophane has a lot of small art galleries, but sometimes I have a hard time keeping up because things open and close pretty quickly.

Fisherman's Wharf

Lavish 19th century Bosphorus mansions and old ferry ports form the foundation of Yeniköy and Emirgan, two neighbourhoods that have suddenly attracted a new wave of cafes, restaurants and bars

| Night | Cocktails and the Bosphorus |

Unlike the other Bosphorus coast neighbourhood of Arnavutköy, where cocktail bars like ANY, Alexandra and Luzia are filled to the brim on weekends, Yeniköy is not quite as notable for its nightlife. However, the opening of *Pero Bar* is changing that and locals appreciate that they now have a cocktail bar within walking distance. Having taken over the first floor of an old Bosphorus home, Pero's back terrace opens up entirely to a full view of the strait, especially enjoyable in the evening when their mixed drinks are accompanied by that subtle summer sea breeze. Signature cocktails include a twist on the Old Fashioned with walnut jam, nut infused rye whiskey and chocolate bitters, or the Saturn Whisper, with pepper infused tequila, elderflower liqueur, rosemary syrup, lime juice, cucumber and aquafaba. Pero is also open during the day as a cafe and restaurant, which means that a full Turkish breakfast or a Pero Burger for lunch are served with the same full-on sea view.
• Pero Bar, Köybası Caddesi Daire Sokak 5A, Yeniköy

House of Art

In 1998 one of Turkey's wealthiest families decided to turn their Bosphorus mansion into a museum. Originally built by the Italian architect Edoardo De Nari in 1925, the *Sakıp Sabancı Museum* was undoubtedly a huge gain for the city's cultural scene. Temporary exhibitions have included works from Rodin, Picasso and Monet, and if that didn't suffice, the museum restaurant is run by the students of MSA, Istanbul's premier culinary school. It's normal to spend a whole day here, wandering the garden, eating, appreciating the sea view from the terrace and admiring art.
• Sakıp Sabancı Museum, Sakıp Sabancı Caddesi 42, Emirgan-Sarıyer

Shop   **Floral Explosion**

It's a good thing that Çagla Yılmaz gave up her job working as a geneticist in pharmaceuticals in order to discover a new calling. She immersed herself in floral design, and after her home atelier began taking over too much space, she opened a shop reflective of all her whims. Potted plants, cut blooms and flower crowns as well as design objects from local artists fill up a space that feels more like a home than a shop. *Mitza* also has its own garden where Yılmaz likes to host events and workshops.
• Mitza, Yarış Sokak 1, Yeniköy

Food   **Catering to Bistro**

The Resitpasa neighbourhood in Emirgan is grad-ually becoming an area of interest with cafes and shops sprouting among the mostly residential streets. One of the leaders is *Aman da Bravo*, which, for many years, was a successful catering company owned by Melis Korkud and Inanç Baykar. Ready for a new challenge, the duo con-verted the space into a bistro where their beauti-ful dishes are first posted on Instagram before they're lovingly devoured. With a seasonal and healthy disposition, a mélange of oven roasted squash, beet and kale with hummus or home-made mandarin ice cream are a common sight.
• Aman da Bravo, Emirgan Sokak 20, Emirgan

Eating In

It's rare to see an entire family home turned into a restaurant, but that's what siblings Burçak and Murat Kazdal did in order to create a space that felt as down-to-earth as their dishes. *Apartıman's* menu reflects Burçak's passion for getting her hands dirty while finding the most seasonal ingredients from independent Turkish producers who share her nature-focused outlook. The three-story Yeniköy restaurant is open all day, as you'd expect of a homely eatery, and in the evenings, wine is replaced with cocktails.
• Apartıman, Köybası Caddesi 153, Yeniköy

Food Female Touch

A veteran of Changa, which once redefined Istanbul's upscale dining scene, talented female chef Pınar Tasdemir has since opened her own restaurant. *Araka's* minimalist interior of exposed brick and decorative gourds is like something out of a magazine, yet its ingeniously prepared and seasonal menu is wholly Turkish with experimental undertones. Think of thinly sliced beetroot in olive oil with creamy Turkish Ezine cheese, or slow cooked lamb with pickled linden flowers. Sip on your glass of boutique Turkish wine in the outside seating area while Tasdemir's pug wanders about curiously.
• Araka, Kappalı Bakkal Sokak 8, Yeniköy

Food Comfort Food

There's nothing elaborate about Kardesim Mantı, a restaurant that many would walk past without a second glance. Decked out like a cozy Anatolian village home, the mother and son team make mantı true to its traditional recipe. The tiny handmade dumplings filled with minced meat are boiled (or fried) and then topped with yogurt, tomato, garlic, melted butter sauce and then sprinkled with various spices. Kardesim's yaprak sarması (stuffed vine leaves) are also notable for being almost as good as any Turkish grandmother's.
• Kardesim Mantı, Doğru Muvakkithane Caddesi 14, Emirgan

Port Stories

Yeniköy's port is a bit to small to accommodate the large and historic Istanbul ferries, but the motor (smaller boat) to Beykoz and back departs from here every half hour. Having maintained its original weathered wood exterior and signpost, the nostalgic port harks back to the days when the Bosphorus was populated by fishermen. Take a few moments to stand by the railing as the boat makes its way from one continent to the other, landing in surprisingly green Beykoz. A five-minute walk from the port, *Muradoglu Balık* is all about the iconic balık ekmek (fish sandwich), as well as fried calamarı and stuffed mussels, which are all served aboard the boat-turned-restaurant. Beykoz's other superb attraction is the *Beykoz Kundura*, a leather shoe factory from the 1920s which was recently converted into a cultural center and cinema. Watch a film from the Kundura Cinema's curated program and walk around the old factory spaces, which were, for many years, used as film sets for especially gritty Turkish soap opera scenes.

• Various locations

Onur Gökhan Gökçek
After leaving behind a career
in ballet he discovered his alter
ego, Nur Topu Saçan, while
working at the local drag queen
temple, Cahide. Since then
she's become a nightlife icon,
performing, DJing and hosting
legendary parties

Onur Gökhan Gökçek, Nightlife Icon

Let the Music Play

A beacon of Istanbul's LGBTQ+ scene with more than ten years of nightlife experience, Gökçek talks about Istanbul's current drag scene explosion, the best queer nightlife spots and who would be on the Turkish version of RuPaul's Drag Race

How did you become a fabulous drag queen?

I started performing on stage about ten years ago, before that it was more of a thing I did at home with friends. I worked at *Cahide* for about five years and after I quit, I went to Switzerland. I worked there for a while and then came back and started working at the nightclub *Love*. Now I'm working freelance and organizing my own parties.

What's the drag scene like in Istanbul?

There's currently a drag queen explosion in Istanbul and I think it's because of the students at Bogaziçi University who are organizing parties and performances amongst each other. There's a really exciting drag scene at the moment with events every weekend, I'm really inspired by the new generation. We're ready to compete with the world!

So where does Istanbul's LGBTQ+ crowd go to party?

Istanbul has a lot of places where the LGBTQ+ crowd can comfortably have a good time. There's a gay bar called *Sahika Teras*, a really sweet venue. There's *Kozmos Café* in Bomonti where we host an event every two weeks with great cocktails and music, with either me playing or a guest DJ. The name of the party I host is 'Jöte Sosyete,' by the way, which throws some shade at all those people who think they're so high society and are not! There's also a place called *Markus Tavern*, which was opened by some friends of ours, they have really great food and cocktails and I sometimes play music there too. There's also a great monthly party called Dudakların Cengi, which is organized by a friend at *Anahit Sahne*, including a drag queen show. *Suma Han* is also a great

nightclub as well as *Gizli Bahçe*. On the Asian side there's *Bina* and *Mecra*.

Do you have any personal Istanbul nightlife favourites?

I used to go to *Minimüzikhol* all the time, you could say I'm a real Minimüzikhol Girl. I was there every weekend and before it was my friend's club, it actually was the first gay club I ever went to, I was 17 and I had my first one night stand there! So, that space has always been very important to me. There's also a new place called *Bonn* in Karaköy, which I really like, I even organized my birthday party there.

How come a lot of places in Istanbul have German names by the way?

There's a bit of a German infatuation going on right now, like a wannabe-Berlin situation. When they opened Bonn, I was wondering why they chose one of Germany's most boring cities, and they said the name just sounded cool. I mean Bonn is very bureaucratic, it's like Ankara, isn't it?

Let's talk a little about fashion, who are your favourite designers, where do you shop?

I actually rarely buy anything new. Sometimes my designer friends will give me clothes, but I mostly try to buy things second-hand because the world already has enough problems with overconsumption. There's the *Bomonti Flea Market*, which is great and cheap, I just bought an amazing pair of shoes there for 10 Turkish Lira. As for designers, there's a guy called Koral Sagular, who is amazing, I'd love to work with him. There's DB Berdan, who I work with, they are very good. I really like the work of Giray Sepin, I'm wearing his creation right now, he's a friend of

With terrace: The restaurant/bar/lounge/atelier Mecra in the bohemian Moda neighborhood

mine! There's also Didem Soydan's shop, *Hole Academie*, which brings some great brands to Turkey.

Walk us through a normal day in the life of Onur.

I'm actually a very domestic person, especially now that I've moved to a bigger place here in Bomonti. So, I definitely don't leave the house when I don't have to. I eat my two eggs for breakfast and then if I have a show coming up, I practice at home and prepare my outfit. But if I have something to do or I want to go out, I usually go to *Kozmos Café*, because a lot of my friends are there. You know, I'm a trendsetter? I moved here and now everyone has started coming here! When I came to Pangaltı and Bomonti ten years ago it was

almost desolate and now it's becoming the new Cihangir, which used to be Istanbul's longstanding boho-cool neighborhood.

Last question, if there was a Turkish RuPaul's Drag Race who would be competing?

Well, I would definitely be RuPaul! There are so many new girls, the first one that comes to mind is Florence Delight, she's very successful at the moment. It would be amazing to round up all the drag queens in Turkey and have them compete against each other.

An Incompatible Love

Feride Yalav-Heckeroth

I moved to Istanbul to the dismay of my parents who wanted me to stay in New York and build a life within the framework of the so-called American Dream. That dream had nothing to offer me. I found myself doing the most touristy thing one could do in Istanbul: sitting at one of those Galata Bridge restaurants and eating balık ekmek.

I watched the old ferries glide by, the lights of Sultanahmet's iconic structures reflected in the dark strait. It was a moment that proved to me how everything surreal is indeed inspired by reality. Istanbul's nostalgia enchanted me. I soon began living between two worlds. The Istanbul I saw, young and new, and the old Istanbul from the grainy photographs of Ara Güler, or scenes from Turkish films from the '60s. I became a little obsessed with Orhan Pamuk's memories and sometimes wished that they were my own, or that I had witnessed a time when the structures that now stood dilapidated were full of life. When Istiklal was the Grand Rue, when people swam on the beaches that lined the Bosphorus, jumped into the water from their mansions. I often wished I had been friends with my father who was a student at Boğaziçi University in the 1970s, that I rode with him in his car up and down the coast. That I was there when the modernists realized their architectural designs. When Atatürk sat in Vefa and drank his boza. I have a hard time adjusting my emotions when Istanbul's past is disrespected, when the landscape is demolished to make way for more apartment buildings which stretch superfluously into the sky, or when I read about Istanbul in the news.

I find myself defending Istanbul to strangers who don't know the city the way I do. And then I give up. And then I return (inevitably) and find instant comfort in the city's young people who, despite it all, continue to do what they love. The chefs and the artists, the shopkeepers and the designers, the drag queens and the entrepreneurs. Something new opens in Istanbul every day; a new event is planned or a new project comes to life like a silent declaration of love for a city that has, for centuries, flourished and fallen and re-emerged. Istanbul is eternal. It's young and brash but also antique and elegant. It's conservative and it's free. Istanbul is a delicate balance that functions despite its opposites. It breaks and it heals.

There was no doubt back in 2011 that Istanbul was on the rise. I took a cab home that night after finishing my balık ekmek. As the driver snaked his way through the narrow streets of Cihangir in order to escape the traffic on the main roads, I was envious of all the young people who sat outside in cafes conversing and drinking, illuminated by the lights inside the old Istanbul apartments, their cigarette smoke rising into the night. They were already locals, so comfortable in their chatter, surrounded by their friends. I immediately found a job as a teacher in an English language centre for adults. They only hired native English speakers, but because I was Turkish yet sounded like an American they decided I would be 'Mia from New York.' I chose that name. Of course, I always broke character and my students appreciated the fact that a Turkish person could also speak 'native' English. I think it kind of gave them hope. I lived in Kadıköy and in the evenings sat on my balcony from where I could see a tiny bit of sea between other buildings. There was an underpass on my street, which was called the 'Feride Geçidi,' and every time I walked through it, I thought that the universe had somehow granted me a sign; that I had made the right decision. But the European side beckoned me as I boarded the ferry and put my feet on the railing while the waves unfolded beneath me. I looked at the other passengers and thought that for those few quiet moments on the Bosphorus we all finally had time to rethink our entire lives. I thought about how Kadıköy had a down-to-earth humility about it, a bohemian spirit that was kind and open. But every time I reached Taksim, I had crossed the strait as if I had crossed the worlds. The ebb and flow of the crowds on İstiklal Street, the high rises of Levent, the ornate 19th century buildings of Pera, the rowdy bars and taverns in Asmalı Mescit, the historic mansions and fancy fish restaurants up and down the wealthy Bosphorus coast…and then Istanbul became my job when I began working for a tourist and expat magazine in one of those Levent towers I had admired from afar. I moved to the European side.

I spent the next two years in the middle of the whirlwind that was the youthful explosion of Istanbul. I ate too much when restaurants invited us to taste their new menus and write reviews. Burrata with a sprinkle of dried tomato, Mille-feuille with raspberries, grilled octopus on a bed of eggplant puree, profiteroles filled with cream, lahmacun with organic ingredients, Turkish breakfast spreads with a view of the Bosphorus, linden pannacotta, passion fruit tarts and Adana kebab. I was the first to write about an American who opened up the city's first real cocktail bar. I collected articles and social media posts and spent my lunch breaks trying out new restaurants and cafes. I wrote neighbourhood profiles and spent days in Balat, Yeniköy, Kuzguncuk and Karaköy wandering the backstreets, discovering old churches and synagogues, art galleries and boutiques, cafes and bars. Old surfaces came to life with the work of the young. I interviewed a street artist who later came to my apartment to draw a giant fox on my wall. On my birthday I drank eight glasses of raki at Ali Haydar tavern and then went to Münferit to order whiskies at the bar as a DJ played music so loud you could barely hear what anyone was saying. We went to Kiki to squeeze through the crowds to get to the terrace where everyone used the excuse of smoking to hit on one another. When the other bars closed but we still hadn't had enough, we ended up at Minimüzikhol, dancing in that tiny space that was once someone's living room. We danced to Justin Timberlake songs on the terrace of Mama Shelter, after rounds of gin & tonics. We climbed on the tables at Lucca and danced to Beyonce, waited in line as groups of people went into the bathrooms to do coke. We ate mantı at 5am and went to bed at 7 and sometimes went to work the next day, unable to function. We stumbled through the streets as the day's first call to prayer reverberated chaotically across the dawn. Watched the sun rise and turn the leaves of plane trees iridescent as we sat on the stairs in front of apartment buildings in Çukurcuma not yet ready to call it a night.

And then Gezi happened, and for the next few weeks we spent our nights on the streets with our water bottles filled with a mixture of liquid antacid and water, meant to mollify the sting of teargas. Taksim turned into a kind of film set with burning police cars and masses of protestors. The streets seemed to be on fire. Everyone helped everyone and nothing felt right except sitting in Gezi Park and just waiting. And when nothing changed, we retreated. And Istanbul did what it does best, life resumed despite any and all circumstances. I left the magazine and became a freelancer, having grown weary of the 9-to-5 boundaries of office life and a boss whose ego-fueled rage threatened to destroy all my fond memories. I travelled as an amateur scriptwriter for a documentary about falconry, and while in Belgium I began to envy something new: a simpler, more predictable life. I fell in love with a German man and moved to Berlin, I got married. But Istanbul never let me go and I kept going back to write articles about eccentric musicians and successful architects, chefs redefining the Turkish kitchen and shopkeepers in love with their craft. And when I do go back to Istanbul I realize that perhaps it wasn't the city that changed, but that it was me who changed. I got older and left and was replaced by a whole new generation of young people filling it with their vivacity, doing the same things that I once did, and maybe doing it better. I'm happy to write about them and to love the city from afar. I suppose like all dysfunctional relationships, absence makes the heart grow fonder.

Feride Yalav-Heckeroth is a writer, editor, and translator based in Berlin and the author behind LOST iN Istanbul. She's written about her city for local and international print and online publications and recently released her own guidebook, 'The 500 Hidden Secrets of Istanbul.'

Aylin Yazıcıoglu
While pursuing a PhD at
Cambridge University she
decided to become a chef at
the age of 36. A Cordon
Bleu degree and a string of
Michelin-starred gigs later,
she's home and helming
Nicole restaurant, atop a for-
mer monastery-turned-hotel.

Aylin Yazıcıoglu, Chef

Kitchen Culture

As chef behind some of Istanbul's most inventive menus, Yazıcıoglu talks about the few local restaurants that really get it right, where she buys her ingredients and what she does in those rare free moments outside the kitchen

You decided to become a chef in your late thirties, can you talk a bit about that?

I was doing a PhD in social history and left in my third year. Of course, I didn't automatically decide to become a chef, I gave myself a year off to figure things out. Food was always a part of my life and my family's, we were always the kind of people who sat down to eat and then continued to talk about food. I became a bit obsessed with gardening and was constantly cooking the ingredients I was growing myself. However, I didn't think that just because I cooked well I could open a restaurant and so I challenged myself by working at a very grimy pub. I told myself that if I could survive that, I could take on the challenge of a professional kitchen. And then I went to school for it.

So, let's talk about Nicole, which is always inspired by seasonal ingredients when it comes to its tasting menu. Where do you get your ingredients?

I try to get ingredients that have travelled as little as possible and I avoid mass produced items. Nothing is harvested in Istanbul anymore so even at the Bomonti Organic Market you get produce from places such as Izmir or Kastamonu, which travel to the city overnight. We like the *Çarşamba Pazarı* (Wednesday Market) in Fatih, one of the larger markets, which has some conventional farming products. We also have a few small producers in Beykoz who grow things in their own gardens. I make an effort to find small producers, so our asparagus comes directly from Eskisehir or our Tulum cheese from a small producer in Bergama. We have a few really great olive oil producers, Zetay from near Manisa, and Mentese SOM from Bodrum.

What about the other restaurants in Istanbul? Any favourite chefs?

Of course. Two of the country's best chefs are definitely Kaan Sakarya and Derin Arıbas who opened *Basta! Street Food Bar* in Moda. I think they've taken fine dining to another level because of their meticulous cooking ethic and how they work with the ingredients. Kaan used to work here at *Nicole*, and he prepares the lamb exactly the same way he did here, except that at Basta he serves it in a dürüm (wrap). Another one is, of course, Civan Er who runs *Yeni Lokanta*. I think he's made a very important contribution to the Turkish kitchen. He refined mantı, for example. He stayed true to its essence, but the taste is extraordinary! There's Emir Inanır, whose restaurant *Aila* I'm excited to try out. I love the meze at *Balat Sahil* Restaurant and their turbot is just excellent. I also love *Jash* in Cihangir, which also opened on Kınalıada (island), you literally step off the ferry and you're in the meyhane, it's right by the port. And for coffee, there's *Petra* which is great.

Where do you go in Istanbul during those rare moments when you're not in the kitchen?

Well I travel to meet with the producers, so the free time I do have is somehow also work-related. But I have started taking sailing lessons at the Kalamıs Sailing Club! It was a childhood dream of mine.

You're also a pastry chef, do you have any tips in terms of classic bakeries in Istanbul?

There's *Palmiye Pastanesi* in Kurtulus, which makes baked goods exactly the way they used to taste in my childhood. They make the classic çatal pastry true to its original recipe with mahalep, and

Unlike its dramatic interior design, the menu at Aila restaurant is rather simple and inspired by traditional Turkish recipes

the sponge cake they make still has mastic inside. But apart from that, I would love for Markiz Pastanesi to go back to its original self. I would love to open Markiz as its former self. There are also a few places that make excellent bread now in Istanbul, for example, *Bröd*, it's a serious bread bakery. There's also *Kruvasan*, which makes good croissants. And *Vakko Patisserie*, that's probably one of the only real patisseries in Istanbul.

And kitchen accessories, where do you shop for those?

We have really great ceramicists. There's Özlem Tuna, she makes jewellery, but also amazing coffee cups. But for plates, bowls etc., there's only Santimetre.

Let's talk a little about wine, where do you go to buy the best?

La Cave is the best place to buy wine, they have the best range in Istanbul. As for wine bars, there are the cafes and bars inside the Tünel Pasajı. There's also *Solera Winery*, which has great wines at very good prices. Plus, there's a great Italian restaurant next door that Solera works with that delivers pizza straight to your table.

Change of Tide

A showcase by Ekin Özbiçer

Granting cinematic transcendence to the quotidian, Özbiçer's ongoing series 'Auto Orientalism' is a perfectly-framed nod to the social and political shifts within Turkey's globalised middle class

Kerem Küçükgürel, Designer

Multi Talented

Kerem Küçükgürel
He is a designer and entrepreneur, a saviour of stray dogs, a collector of vintage Ken dolls and the ultimate host. Co-creator of the gentleman's fashion house and atelier Civan, Küçükgürel creates men's collections that are inspired by the elegance of the past. Floral bow ties, bespoke pin-stripe suits in sun-kissed yellows, sailor hats, and polka dot shirts are all part of Civan's seemingly endless charm.

Whilst sipping champagne and nibbling candied chestnuts in his atelier and shop in Galata, Kerem Küçükgürel shared his favourites from the new generation of Istanbul entrepreneurs, the city's few remaining artisans and certain spots that continue to exude nostalgia

Can you talk a little about how a unique fashion house like Civan came to be?

We opened Civan with Bahar Gözkün who's a very old friend of mine. Back in the day she went to Holland to study and when I went to visit her, we ended up crazily scouring an Amsterdam flea market one Saturday morning. We found a beautiful button-down shirt that was made here in Beyoglu. We didn't say anything to each other, but the thoughts were percolating. A few months later I sent her the idea and story for Civan, and the building I found for our first atelier. Bahar decided to come back to Istanbul. I bought all our equipment and sewing machines from Paris and Civan began. In Turkey, men are usually introduced to the tailor-made suit either when they're graduating or getting married, so we had a special ceremony suits collection. We also create entire wardrobes for some of our customers. So at the moment we're quite busy, we're constantly producing.

What are some of you favorite nostalgic venues in Istanbul?

We love Rejans restaurant which reopened as *1924 Istanbul*. We shop a lot in the *Avrupa Pasajı* as well as the *Bomonti Flea Market*. I also love the patisserie *Inci Pastanesi* and there's the Umay Kundura (shoemaker) right across from them who makes these amazing dance shoes! There's the Nazaryan Kundura in Nisantası who is also a legend.

Where do you get your fabrics and vintage accessories?

We buy our buttons in Paris. Our shoes are from Erten Ivme, Beyoglu's oldest shoemaker, he's 87 years old and has made shoes for everyone including Zeki Müren. We make our own bow ties and we buy a lot of vintage fabrics, the eskiciler

(second-hand sellers) bring them to us. Turkey still produces great fabrics, but we also get some from Italy.

So, let's talk about the new generation of Istanbul entrepreneurs, who are your favourites?

Let me start with *A Hidden Bee* which is great for women's clothing. I really like *Noce Home* for furniture and home accessories. I like *Bago*, she makes fantastic bags. I go to the juice bar *PO Juicery* very often, everything they make is delicious. I'm obsessed with *Homemade Aromaterapi* and Safiye Sabun and their 100% natural beauty products. They just opened a new shop in Nisantası. For ceramics, *Santimetre*, forever. For flowers, *Vesaire* in Tesvikiye, when she creates a bouquet, it's like she's reading your soul. *Pero* bar, and not just because I did their logo, but also because their cocktails are amazing. There's *Kaia*, the restaurant and bar belonging to Gökhan Kusoglu who's one of the best mixologists. And for sweet things I love *Minia* which was opened by Esra Evci Atay. She makes amazing products, even vegan and flourless. I also love *Ek Biç Ye Iç*, a restaurant and urban farming collective near my house.

You've also dabbled a bit in the restaurant scene. What are your favourite places to eat in Istanbul?

I think I'm a bit old school, but I love *Journey* and *Mangerie*. When I'm in the mood for sushi I go to Ioki. *Mikla* restaurant is still a classic for me. Definitely *Binevideli* in Etiler, I love their vegan dishes. When I feel like fresh fish, *Maria's Restaurant* in Etiler.

A minimal library of natural beauty products: soaps, candles, oils, creams and shampoos at Safiye Sabun

Binevideli
Etiler

Maria's Restaurant
Etiler

Sanayi 313
Maslak

Baska Sinema
Beyoglu

Any cool Istanbul designers that inspire you?

I really like the work of Enis Karavil, who established the concept store *Sanayi 313*. I also love the new illustrators, one of my favourites is Sedat Girgin who we've been working with on a Civan illustration.

Where do those special grooms who wear bespoke Civan suits for their wedding get married by the way?

They love rural weddings, so a lot of weddings on the Aegean and Mediterranean coast and islands. In Istanbul, they get married at Cezayir restaurant, Fransız Bahçeleri (French Gardens in Tarabya), the Aslı Tunca Hotel, and Aija Hotel. As one of the most interesting weddings, we have a couple who's marrying at the Cumhuriyet Meyhane (tavern).

The truly hand-made are always imperfect. Ceramics at the mindful women's clothing boutique A Hidden Bee

Bomonti Organic Market
Bomonti

UniqIstanbul
Maslak

What do you do when you get off work?

Sometimes I go to the cinema and watch about three to four movies in a row. The old Beyoglu Cinema now hosts *Baska Sinema*, which brings the best independent and arthouse films to Istanbul. I go to the *Bomonti Organic Market* on Saturday and the Bomonti Flea Market on Sunday. I think if I didn't live in Gümüssuyu, I would definitely live in Bomonti. For concerts we go to *UniqIstanbul*.

You have a very unique style, where do you feel at home in Istanbul?

There are a few places where I feel at home. One of them is Georges Hotel and the other is Cezayir Restaurant. I like the 360 Restaurant and I really like the French Cultural Center in Taksim, they always have great films. I love the Pera Palace and the Büyük Londra Hotel. I like Rıfat Özbek's design pillow store Yastık. For vintage shops, Şamdan Antik in Çukurcuma is my go-to place. Modern Tarih is also legendary for antiques. I really like Oytun Berktan, both as a showroom and an interior design office. And the Marmara Hotel's chocolate shop.

Behold the Young

Once the homebase of prominent Greek Orthodox families during the Ottoman era, the endearingly dilapidated Balat and Fener neighbourhoods are coming back to life through Istanbul's young and ingenious entrepreneurs with their stylish cafes, restaurants and galleries

Food	Simple Treats

The charm of Istanbul relies heavily on its back street eateries. *Köfteci Arnavut* (pictured) is one of these institutions. Opened in 1947, it's still in daily operation, with a weathered-wood interior and small maritime antiques hanging on the walls. Köfteci Arnavut (as the name implies) is the place to eat charcoal-grilled köfte (meatballs) accompanied by ayran (a drink made of yogurt), piyaz (bean vinaigrette salad) and a couple of slices of bread. Another back street favorite is *Çanak Mangalda Kurufasulye*, a restaurant that has been making the traditional Turkish comfort food kurufasulye (bean stew) true to its original recipe for years. The kurufasulye is cooked on a coal fire for 4–5 hours, hence its signature taste and texture and is (upon order) topped with slices of pastırma (cured spiced beef) and accompanied by tursu (mixed pickled vegetables). Don't forget to order a bowl of their thick yogurt made from water buffalo milk, which is, for many Turkish people, a sauce that goes with every warm dish.

• Various locations

Semt Pazarı

Every major neighbourhood in Istanbul has its own semt pazarı (neighbourhood market) that sets up stalls on specific days. Sellers with goods from all over Turkey arrive at these markets and some of the most popular ones include the very natural *Bomonti Organic Market* (Saturdays) and the gigantic *Fatih Market* (Wednesdays). Balat also has its own little neighbourhood market (pictured) every Tuesday. Pop by to procure fresh produce as well as cheeses, village bread, olives, herbs, nuts and the famous Tasköprü garlic.
• Various Locations

Culture   New Life

The opening of new venues in Balat and Fener have been a boon for the area because of the consequent refurbishment of its distinct architecture. Original tile flooring and wooden details have gained new life and purpose in modern cafes such as the Kinfolk-inspired *Cooklife Balat* and third-wave coffee leader *Coffee Department*. *Artlocalist* (pictured) kept the original brick walls for its café and renovated the winding staircase, which leads up to an art gallery/events space. With carefully selected design objects and furniture, the neighbourhood revival has become a confluence of old and new.
• Various locations

Food   Until Late

Most Istanbul people head to the meyhanes (taverns) in Asmalı Mescit when they want to spend an evening drinking rakı and eating meze with close friends. But only a few true meyhane lovers spend their evenings in Balat, basking in the nostalgia of this very classic restaurant that's hasn't changed much since opening around 1991. Above par dishes include marinated sea bream, stuffed onions, Sinop-style liver and a rather legendary grilled turbot, which all pair well with many glasses of cold rakı.
• Balat Sahil Restaurant,
Mürselpasa Caddess 245, Balat

The Red Castle

It's impossible to miss the *Fener Rum Erkek Lisesi* (Phanar Greek Orthodox Boys' Lyceum), which kind of hovers over the neighbourhood in a striking shade of dark red. Still operational with a small student population, the school was first established in 1454 and went on to become the city's most prestigious Greek Orthodox educational facility. Just behind the Lyceum, on Tevkii Cafer Mektebi Street, is *Yuvakimyon*, a former Greek Orthodox Girls' School, which sporadically hosts art exhibitions in its beautiful old rooms.
• Various Locations

Outdoors Serene Waters

Steering away from the mainstream-tour-operator approach is what has made Sinan Sökmen and his company Istanbul Tour Studio so successful. Think of an Istanbul food tour curated by Vogue Turkey's Food Editor, a helicopter ride for a comprehensive bird's-eye-view of the city, or mushroom hunting in the Belgrade Forest. Of course, nothing beats waking up early in the morning to enjoy the serenity of the Golden Horn with a private rowing lesson. Be prepared to feel a little sore the next day, but it's worth it for the view of Balat and Fener from the water.
• Istanbul Tour Studio, istanbultourstudio.com

Food Noma to Balat

After studying in America and working at Noma in Copenhagen, Sinan Bakkaloğlu returned to Istanbul to open his own restaurant in Balat. At a brave distance from the other cafes, Smelt & Co has the street to itself (for now). Homemade Kombucha and ingenious dishes made from seasonal ingredients create heavenly taste combinations that you'd otherwise never find in this neighbourhood. The restaurant's beautiful plates are also worth a separate mention, handmade by Chloris Ceramic.
• Smelt & Co, Kiremit Caddesi 16A, Balat

| Factory Art Space

Amateur photographers love wandering around Balat and Fener, because of the run-down apartments that still exude the elegance of their past. Suela J. Cennet must have been equally enchanted when she transformed a former generator factory into an art museum, calling it *The Pill* (pictured). The former Director of the Daniel Templon Gallery in Paris-Brussels, Cennet has successfully maintained the gallery as a minimalist space for multidisciplinary contemporary art from local and international artists. Past exhibitions have included paintings by the Franco-Polish artist Apolonia Sokol, the sculptural work of French contemporary artist Daniel Firman and paintings by Turkish artist Leyla Gediz. Another dilapidated space that gained a second life is the atelier of Bürkan Özkan who is one of the few remaining sign writers left in Istanbul. Özkan's *Klasik Tabela Atölyesi* (Classic Signboard Atelier) is a traditional sign painting, branding and graphic design studio that has already bestowed more than a few Istanbul venues with signboards inspired by the city's old-school typeface aesthetic.

• Various locations

Yaprak Aras & Alican Tezer
Yaprak Aras used to work as a fashion editor for Vogue Turkey before she co-founded the bespoke concept store Souq Dükkan, which originally began as a themed vintage bazaar. Her long-term boyfriend Alican Tezer is mostly known for being the drummer of the band Büyük Ev Ablukada, alongside various other musical side projects. The creative couple lives together in Karaköy.

Yaprak Aras & Alican Tezer, Entrepreneur & Musician

Perfect Match

Through their busy life of fashion, craft, recording studios and concert halls, Yaprak and Alican enjoy the bustling inner city life of Istanbul as well as travelling the world. To relax, they escape to the forests and beaches around the Turkish megapolis

You have diverse backgrounds, how did you meet?

Yaprak: We had mutual friends. We became really good friends at first.

Alican: I mean really really good friends, like wingmen.

Why do you live in Karaköy?

Alican: Our music studio with Büyük Ev Ablukada was in that area and I've been living there for over ten years and know everyone.

Yaprak: We also started organizing our themed bazaars in the same two-storey building, downstairs in a space that looked like a warehouse. Souq soon turned into a store, Souq Dükkan, and even though we moved it to Kanyon a few years later we still live in Karaköy. Our apartment is next to a historical building, *Tophane-i Amire*, which was built by the famous architect Mimar Sinan as a canon factory. Nowadays it's mostly used for art shows.

What are your favourite breakfast and lunch spots in town?

Yaprak: *Journey* is very close to our place and we often go there for breakfast. It's simply the first venue that comes to mind when we think about food in our neighbourhood. They serve a modern menu in a very laid-back atmosphere. I love *Mangerie* for brunch, the chef, Elif Yalın, is a friend and the place has a very nice view. I go to *The Allis* at Soho House, especially when the weather is nice, and like to sit in the garden. *Petra* is a coffee brand that owns a few places in town, but their headquarters in Gayrettepe is a huge and beautiful place.

Alican: When it comes to coffee, *Norm* is also a great meeting point in our neighbourhood. For lunch, I love burgers and even though there are a lot of burger places in town, *Zula* is really outstanding. They

have two locations. I prefer the one in Kanyon where our shop is now. It's a small place and they only offer three types of burgers, but they're all great.

Yaprak: I love *Bi Nevi Deli*. They serve Istanbul's best plant-based food. *Delicatessen* in Nisantası is also on our list for lunch. In my opinion, it's the best spot in the Nisantası area for food.

Alican: *Basta! Street Food Bar* is on the other side of Istanbul, and they serve modern street food. *Karaköy Lokantası* and *Mana* in Karaköy are our classic spots when someone comes to town for lunch and dinner.

Alican, as a musician what are the hottest venues in town for local underground music?

Alican: If you are asking about the real underground, the first name that comes to mind is, of course, *Peyote*. It has been the most important place that reflects Istanbul's underground scene. On the other side, I mean the Asian side, there is *Arkaoda* and *Bina*. Arkaoda recently opened a place in Berlin too. Bina is a meeting point for the Kadıköy music and art scene and apart from gigs and concerts, they also host exhibitions, movie screenings and talks.

Who are the young Istanbul musicians or bands to keep an eye on?

Alican: They're not all young, but they are new. Gülin is a very good contemporary singer/songwriter, all her songs are very unique, that's what I love most about her, and that her songs always tell a story. Özgür Yılmaz is one of my all-time favourites, he is a very good guitarist who has Spanish, Aegean and Anatolian melodies in his songs. Brek has been catching my attention these days, they have nice synth sounds and look good on

Specially chosen and wholly representative of local talent: Souq Dükkan in Kanyon

stage. Some other names that I admire are Anadol, Gaye Su Akyol, Ezhel, Palmiyeler, Özer Bey, Lin Pesto, Seha Can and Barıs K.

Yaprak, you run one of the most bespoke concept stores in town and know the market, when it comes to fashion, who are your favourite local designers currently?

Yaprak: Nackiye is a pretty new ready-to-wear womenswear brand founded by two sisters. I like their vision and all of their collections so far, they combine traditional elements with contemporary designs. I like Rumisu, an accessories brand, also by two sisters, which we have in our store. They make great scarves and ready-to-wear collections with witty illustrations that tell stories, each piece is like wearable art, both elegant and fun. Another new one is Faraway, a ready-to-wear brand inspired by the designer Ayse Boyner's travels, I really love her taste. Bornn Enamelware launched their brand at one of our bazaars so they are very close to our hearts. They're available all around the world now, including Merci Paris, Selfridges, MOMA Design Store and more.

When not in your own shop, where do you go shopping?
Yaprak: We have over 200 brands, so I mostly do my shopping at our store, but I do go to other shops for the atmosphere. I'm actually not a person who likes to shop a lot, but I love *Fey*, it's owned by one of my former bosses: Fatos Yalın, she was the first fashion editor in Turkey. And then there's *Müz*, the best botanical store in town. They offer plants, pottery, accessories and have a cafe inside. I like *Wohha* for pottery – we used to sell her work, but now she runs her own store including an atelier with ceramic classes. Other places on my list are *Minoa* for books, *Der Liebling Atelier* for jewellery and *Junk* for vintage home design.
Alican: I mostly do record shopping in Istanbul and my favorite shops are *Deform*, *Analog Kültür* and *Kontra Plak*.

Where do you enjoy sitting outside in the sun?
Alican: We go to the forest with our friends for picnics and some-times to barbecue. We usually end up in Belgrad Ormanı.
Yaprak: It's always good to be on the ferry if the sun is shining. There's *Maçka Park*, close to our place and walking by the Bosphorus is always relaxing, especially between Arnavutköy and Bebek with a beautiful view.
Alican: And if it is really hot, we like going to the beaches close to Kilyos on the Black Sea.

Where would you go to spend a romantic day and evening?
Yaprak: We would escape the city and go to the Prince Islands. We love Burgaz, one of the smallest ones. We'd have a rakı-balık (raki-fish) dinner and spend the weekend there.

What is the perfect soundtrack for a boat ride on the Bosphorus?
Alican: My Bosphorus soundtracks differ from time to time. Recently, Frankie Reyes goes well with the boat rides. You can listen to Anadol's Uzun Havalar and of course my all time favourite, Dead Combo from Portugal.

Wohha in Bebek creates distinguishable ceramics with personality

Some trips
for bad

re too short
meals.

Make sure they're
all good with the LOST iN app.

Mixed Media

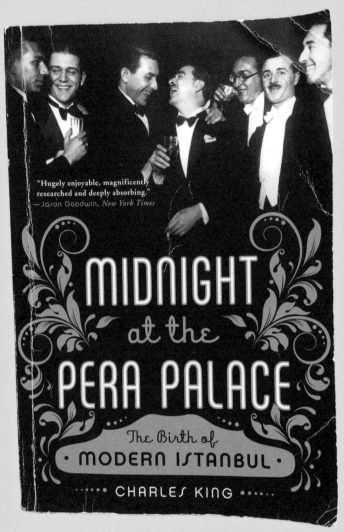

"Hugely enjoyable, magnificently researched and deeply absorbing."
— Jason Goodwin, *New York Times*

MIDNIGHT at the PERA PALACE

The Birth of MODERN ISTANBUL

CHARLES KING

Midnight at the Pera Palace
• Charles King, 2014

King presents a multitude of personal stories that weave together a portrait of Istanbul in the interwar era, a city without borders filled with artists and jazz musicians, spies and exiles. A marvellous introduction to Istanbul's multifaceted essence.

Books

Architecture in Translation
• Esra Akcan, 2012

Esra Akcan explores the concept of translation in the visual field by focusing on the modern city architecture of German-speaking Turkish architects from the 1920s to the 1950s. A fascinating show-case of Turkey's architectural landscape and its changes through the eras with a tight exploration of German influence.

Ara Güler's Istanbul
• Ara Güler, 2009

Known as 'The Eye of Istanbul,' Ara Güler is Turkey's most promi-nent photojournalist whose black-and-white city portraits from the '50s and '60s are among his most important work. This melancholic collection of Istanbul moments includes an introduction by the Nobel Prize winning author Orhan Pamuk.

Films

**Crossing the Bridge:
The Sound of Istanbul**
• Fatih Akın, 2005

Akın follows German musician Alexander Hacke as he travels through Istanbul meeting and jamming with some of the city's most important musicians. From rap to Anatolian rock to legendary arabesque, Akın's documentary offers an unfiltered glimpse into Istanbul's musical core.

Kedi
• Ceyda Torun, 2016

Istanbul belongs to its street cats. This documentary follows the daily lives of seven felines as they expertly traverse the city and interact with their chosen humans.

Uzak
• Nuri Bilge Ceylan, 2002

Set against the melancholic greys of Istanbul in winter, Ceylan's lens subtly portrays the utter discon-nect between two cousins from wholly different backgrounds who unsuccessfully attempt to regain their spirit for life.

Music

34 Oto Sanayi
• BaBa ZuLa, 2014

BaBa ZuLa's eighth album is a journey through experimental sounds and improvisation inspired by Turkey's psychedelic music of the '60s as well as a confluence of traditional Turkish and Balkan instruments and electronica.

Fantezi Müzik
• Jakuzi, 2017

Jakuzi's first album was only released as a cassette in 2016 but was quickly picked up by a record company and re-released in 2017 with new tracks. Since then, the duo has become the leader of Istanbul's synth-wave scene.

Marsandiz
• Hey Douglas, 2019

Alongside the likes of heavy hitters such as Barış K., Hey Douglas is a DJ who has helped revive Turkey's psychedelic, funk and soul songs of the 1960s and 1970s. His first album shows off his skills in remixing and sampling to make the old new again.

Palace of Dwarves

Palace of Dwarves

Engin Türkgeldi

"There must be some kind of way out of here, said the joker to the thief"
All Along the Watchtower, Bob Dylan

"Along with these, there was at one time a dwarves' house in Üsküdar. This house, which was built for dwarves, not for ordinary people, was perfectly complete."
Orhan Pamuk, Silent House

I was twelve years old when my father sold me to Ibrahim Agha. It was three months prior to the circumcision celebration of the Sultan's son. The scoundrel who called himself my father had heard that the celebration was in need of jesters and freaks and brought me to the Agha, who was a distant relative.

"You know of our biggest son, Agha?" he asked. "And by 'biggest,' I mean the first born," he said with a wide grin that exposed his dirty teeth.

"For years we never uttered the word, 'dwarf,' we fed him even when we couldn't feed ourselves, quenched his thirst before ours. We didn't separate him from his healthy siblings. Without any retribution, without expecting the smallest deed. We accepted him as the commendation of our posterity. But when he became mute after a seizure last year, his mother's heart couldn't bear to see him in his frail state. The poor woman's heart is already weak. I'm afraid that one day when she looks at this mute dwarf and sighs in agony she'll keel over and leave my three young children orphaned."

The weather was hot. I was sweating. The tripe soup smell emanating from my father made me sick to my stomach. As instructed, I had bowed my head. But, unable to control myself, I did throw a few wayward glances. From the expression on Ibrahim Agha's face it was clear that he didn't believe a word my father was uttering, but he continued to listen silently anyway, without interrupting. As if emboldened by Ibrahim Agha's disinterest and my forced silence, my prick of a father continued embellishing his elaborate lies.
"We've visited every doctor, consulted every hodja, tried every spell. My Agha, there's no remedy. If it was up to me, I'd never let him go, he's my son after all, but his mother's health is a matter of concern. And while we were busy seeking a cure, everything we owned melted away. My work isn't going so well anyway."

With the play for sympathy concluded, the sales pitch began. He took a breath. Wiped his sweat. Looked at me innocently. Stroked my head. It was clear that he had rehearsed this very scene.

"He may be a dwarf and a mute, but he knows how to behave properly, show respect and obey. Plus, he's not deaf. And I've heard that our Sultan is particularly fond of dwarves and that mutes are always in his presence. This boy is both a dwarf and a mute, you won't be able to find anything better."

I raised my head and stared at that prick who had entwined himself in idiotic arrogance. Just as he was about to open his mouth once more Ibrahim Agha stuck his hand in his waistcloth. He pulled out a velvet pouch, placed the coins into the swindler's hand. I stood on my toes but couldn't see into the crook's open palm. I didn't see for how much I had been sold. My father planted a fake kiss on my forehead. That was the last time I saw him.

I began to walk toward the palace with Ibrahim Agha. It felt as if the weather had gotten colder. He put his hand on my shoulder, "That seizure was a lie. You've become a mute from being beaten, haven't you?" he asked. I looked at the ground. He didn't say anything. When we arrived at the main entrance the guards lowered their spears. The giant gate opened as if by magic. We went inside. The gate closed behind us silently with the same spell.

***

Ibrahim Agha took me to Seker Efendi, the head of the court jesters. He took him aside and whispered something in his ear. I saw the velvet pouch appear for a moment then disappear. But I wasn't sure who had given and who had received the coins. Seker Efendi returned and took me to my room. He gave me two outfits made from Thessaloniki fabric. When he saw me inspecting my new garments he said, "Don't worry. It will fit. After all, you're all the same: small." His golden tooth shone for a brief moment.

He took me to my room. Everything looked like it was from the 'Palace of Dwarves,' a fable that my grandmother used to tell me. Tiny beds, tiny stools, wardrobes for my height. I thought, "so this is how the others live." I so relished this space made specially for my measurements, that in the following days I would look around and imagine that the whole world was like this. That everyone was my height and all the furniture was made for my size. No one spoke. The whole world was this room. Small and silent.

I quickly learned the palace's daily operations. Seker Efendi would gather all of us dwarves and the other jesters in the forecourt and distribute us according to the day's tasks: entertaining the Pashas who came to the palace, clowning around for the children of the Sultan's Chief Consorts, adding amusement to a rowboat outing...The Sultan's favourites, however, would wait at the inner courtyard, ready to humor him at whim. Not that duties outside the familiar, such as posing for portraits by European envoys, did not sometimes occur. However, the only events that all the jokers looked forward to were the celebrations. The tips given out at celebrations such as Palace weddings, births or conquests were always much larger than usual. Not to mention the opportunity to leave the accustomed routine for the chance to show ourselves off.

One year after entering the palace, this kind of celebration allowed me to become one of the Sultan's favourites. The Sultan very much enjoyed my impression of the Alexandrian Cripple Fethi Pasa, which I performed at the celebration organized for the wedding of his youngest sister. He gave Seker Efendi the order that I would stand ready in the inner courtyard and not be sent anywhere else.

The day after the wedding, with the crowds dispersed, the Sultan requested his favourite jesters to the poolside. He made me perform my impression of the Alexandrian Cripple Fethi Pasa once more and laughed heartily. Upon request I also did an impression of Seker Efendi.

A wrestling match was organized between the dwarves. I won. Then they made me fight two other dwarves at the same time and I won again. It was only when the Sultan called me to his side for my tip that he realized that I was a mute. I knew that our sovereign possessed a special fondness for mutes. The essence of his fondness was not mercy but comfort. It wasn't suitable for a grand ruler to have elongated chats with his inferiors, whereas with his mutes, he could sustain long conversations easily through sign language. He asked me how long I had been at the palace and what my family did for a living. He said I fought well for a dwarf. I didn't tell him of my burning desire to fight the members of my former home.

"Every day I carried sheep larger than my size for my father's butcher shop, my Sultan," I answered with sign language.

From that day forth, the Sultan frequently called me to his side. Alongside the impressions, wrestling and water tricks that he liked, I also performed specially requested knife and magic tricks. Sometimes when the other dwarves performed, he made me sit by his feet as he signed to me.

One time he asked what it was like to be a dwarf.
"It's wonderful, my Sultan. My world is larger than everyone else's," I said.
He grew angry.
"Don't give me a fool's answer! Tell me the truth. I command it," he yelled. The jesters surrounding him stopped for a few seconds and then continued their performance as if nothing had happened. I noticed the dirty grins of the jokers who were particularly envious of me. I realized that the Sultan was not testing me.

"My highness, being a dwarf," I said with my hands shaking, "is like constantly being in the wrong place. Always in someone else's home." I swallowed.

"You know where you would feel at home, dwarf? In the Palace of Dwarves." I threw my head back and opened my mouth like I was laughing because I thought he was joking.

"Stop laughing. Don't you believe in the existence of the Palace of Dwarves?" I stayed still. I didn't know how to answer.

"Far from it...who am I to doubt the words of our Sultan? I thought that the Palace of Dwarves was an imaginary place, I was wrong. Forgive me."

"Of course there's a Palace of Dwarves. In fact, if you continue obeying me, I will consider assigning you there as a delegate," he signed. I couldn't help but stare at him for a few moments. I was very confused. The Sultan suddenly burst out laughing.

"There's still time until then. Come on, do your Cripple Fethi impression once more and cheer us up."

Without saying another word, I took a broken branch from the base of the plane tree, pulled my hood sideways and began to limp. The sultan convulsed with laughter.

***

I didn't see the Sultan for a long time. He had gone on an expedition. In his absence, I went wherever Seker Efendi sent me. But I constantly thought about the Sultan's words. Could the Palace of Dwarves, which I had accepted as a fairytale, be real? I couldn't research in books or maps for I was illiterate. Even if I could read and write they would have never allowed me into the library. I couldn't trust the other jesters. They might have lied on purpose because of their envy. I was hesitant to ask anyone else. I didn't want to divulge, but at the same time I was writhing with relentless curiosity. One time I tried to unburden myself to Ibrahim Agha.

"Try focusing on your own palace instead of thinking about some other foreign place!" he rebuffed, as he evaded the subject. "Seker Efendi says that you're not as amusing anymore. You haven't prepared any new performances. And during two of your knife-trick shows you cut your hand. Come to your senses. Pull yourself together before the Sultan comes back."

The Sultan was in rather low spirits when he returned from his excursion at the end of Spring.

There were various rumors. The lack of spoils, unrest brought upon by some Pashas, the incompetence of his son, his favourite mare being put down because of a broken leg...The Sultan rarely summoned us to the poolside and when he did, he appeared subdued and indifferent. One evening, as I pulled my hood sideways and prepared to hobble on an imaginary cane to cheer up the Sultan, he suddenly yelled, "Don't you dare do that cripple impression or I will have your head." From that day on I only performed practical jokes, wrestling and water tricks like the other dwarves. I feared that my relationship with the Sultan would never be the same and that the Palace of Dwarves would not be mentioned again.

When I was about to give up all hope, Seker Efendi told me that the Sultan had summoned me. He hadn't summoned anyone else; strange. With my heart racing, I appeared before our sovereign. He sat cross-legged on the divan. In his hand was a bright red apple. He ordered the others to leave the room. On his face was a smile I had never seen before.

"Dwarf, I want the Cripple Fethi," he said.
"My Lord you said that if I ever did his impression again..."
"I don't want his impression, I want his head, dwarf."
I was bewildered. Had I heard him correctly?
"My Highness, I'm just a simple jester, not an executioner. Besides..."
"I know what you are, dwarf. But this is a different kind of task. Otherwise I would have already summoned that cursed creature to the palace and laid him under the executioner's axe."
He stood up.
"This is not for you to know, but I'm only telling you to prevent any hesitation when you kill him. He's a traitor who is plotting against me and his influence has lately increased. It might cause a stir if he's openly executed in the palace.

That's why the task falls upon you. Plus, the Alexandrian Fethi is a senile loon. And he's a cripple. Even a dwarf like you can take him on."

He came closer and fastened his dark eyes on mine.

"Next week is his daughter's wedding. You will go to his palace with a special performance and do away with him. The executioner will tell you the rest," he said. As I walked backwards toward the entrance, he said:

"Dwarf, if you succeed at this," and took a bite from his apple. "If you succeed, you can wish anything of me."

I don't know whether it was the herb that the executioner gave me for courage, but the wedding night was like a hazy hallucination. A dream one can only remember in fragments. I remember coming to the mansion. How the men formed a circle in the Selamlık. Bottle jugglers, monkey tamers, musicians. The laughter as my turn came to perform. Colourful lanterns, heat, the smell of tripe soup. The dancers and musicians that would perform after me. The tight-rope walker who waited on the side. How Cripple Fethi Pasha stood up and began to limp down that long and dark corridor. How I came up close behind him, how I pulled on his garb. How I tried to tell him, with the signature exaggerated gestures of a jester, that I wanted to perform a trick for him. How he didn't understand but grinned sweetly at the joker before him. Then how I snatched his cane and suddenly hit his good leg with all my strength. How he fell to his knees, his bad leg unable to bear the weight. I remember how he was my height then. How I pulled the knife from the waistcloth of my costume, how I stepped behind him and cut his throat, the spurting blood, the wheezing sounds he made. And how he grinned even when he fell to the ground.

***

The executioner was waiting for me underneath the linden tree in Sarayburnu. He had said that I should hide for a while since it was dangerous to return to the palace immediately after the murder. I was soaked in sweat.

"Did you take care of it?" he asked. I nodded.

"You joker, you!" he smiled. "Did you decide what you'll ask from our Sultan?" I nodded again.

Just then I heard a crackle behind me. Then a rope being pulled taut. I closed my eyes. On the horizon the famous golden domes of the Palace of Dwarves appeared.

Engin Türkgeldi is a doctor by profession who released his first collection of short stories entitled 'Orada Bir Yerde,' (Somewhere Over There), this year. His tales often travel to the more fantastic realms in order to explore universal human truths.

Also available from LOST iN

… and Austin, Dusseldorf, Edinburgh, Helsinki, Oslo, Porto, Reykjavik, Rotterdam, Seattle, Tangier, Tel Aviv in the LOST iN Mobile App.

LOSTIN.COM